YOU CAN BEGIN AGAIN

When The Relationship Meet Unbearable Pain

YOU CAN BEGIN AGAIN

When The Relationship Meet Unbearable Pain

Doretha B. John

XULON PRESS

Xulon Press
2301 Lucien Way #415
Maitland, FL 32751
407.339.4217
www.xulonpress.com

Due to the changing nature of the Internet, if there are any web addresses,
links, or URLs included in this manuscript, these may have been altered
and may no longer be accessible. The views and opinions shared in this
book belong solely to the author and do not necessarily reflect those of the
publisher. The publisher therefore disclaims responsibility for the views or
opinions expressed within the work.

Unless otherwise indicated, Scripture quotations taken from the King James
Version (KJV) – *public domain*.

Paperback ISBN-13: 978-1-66282-685-6
Ebook ISBN-13: 978-1-66282-686-3

I am a survivor! I survived the storm! You can and you will begin again!

Sometimes life is not the way we planned. But regardless of our situations and circumstances, we can pick up the pieces bit by bit and begin again!

"I am strong because I've been weak; I am fearless because I've been afraid; I am wise because I've been foolish." Motivational Quotes.com

CHAPTER 1

I was born and raised in a small southern farm community. I was born a Baptist baby, and growing up, I worshipped as a Baptist member and served as a church usher, a Sunday school teacher, a choir member, and an assistant secretary—all before I was eighteen years old! According to the adults, in the church, at school and home, I was always considered a leader because I didn't wait to be told when I saw a need. So, I was close to most grown-ups, who taught me a lot of things that I later found out were unrealistic.

I was born in an era where women existed to be seen and not heard. My grandmother, who I called Mama, and my grandfather, who I called Daddy, raised me, so I was taught what they knew. My grandfather was the rooster of the coop, and what he said and did was what was! Daddy knew we disliked getting up at 5:00 a.m. every morning for prayer, but Mama did it because that was what he wanted. We would meet in the family room and kneel in prayer seven days a week, 365 days a year! I know now that this was a great and disciplined way to show humbleness to God, but when you're young, you don't think that way. You just know that getting up at 5:00 a.m. every morning to pray is horrible. Of course, years later, I found out that those prayers were the ones that kept us!

CHAPTER 2

Mama had no say over anything. Oh, I'm sorry...she did make decisions on what to cook and how to clean the house! Mama was very protective of me, and she spoiled me. She never asked me to do any cooking or washing, but only limited household duties. Daddy didn't have a male in the house, since my uncle was in the Army, so he used the two girls, (my cousin and me) in the house to help with the harvest of the crops.

So, that was my environment. I didn't have the luxury of most comforts, but for the most part, I was happy and content knowing that I was very much loved! We were the well-respected family in the community. Everybody came to Daddy for help. Be it prayer, encouraging words, a ride downtown, or financial help, he was the one they called.

When it came to my choice of friends, Daddy was very strict, so I had a restricted social life. At the time, I didn't like the restrictions, but I discovered years later that Daddy was right. I learned that what happens in our lives depends on who we keep company with, where we spend our time, who we live with, and most importantly, who we let feed our mind.

I was very fortunate to have grandparents who believed that education was an important factor in life. When others in the community were keeping their children home to help harvest the crops, Daddy made sure I was in school. He always said that he would make sure I earned an education because I was not farm material!

After high school, I could not wait to leave home and pursue my dream of becoming a Clinical Psychologist, which required many years of study. Thankfully, I was awarded a two-year state scholarship. Getting married was not in my plan, even if I was being pursued by two men. I was determined to fulfill my dream of a higher education.

CHAPTER 3

When I was sixteen years old, I met my future husband. Most Saturdays and Sundays, but usually on Sunday evenings after church, I would visit my aunt and her family, who lived just down the road from our house. I would gather with her children and other neighboring children, and we would laugh and have fun together. Because my aunt's house was located on the main highway, we could see all the traffic that came by. That is how I met my husband. He was driving by and saw us girls standing by, and he stopped! He and I started talking, and that was the beginning of our courtship. Since he was in the military, I only got to see him once a week. After about six to eight months of dating, he was shipped out to Japan. However, he continued to communicate with me through mail. Sometimes I would even get letters twice in one week! He would also send me gifts from Japan.

I got married over the objection of my family, because my life was going in the right direction and marriage was not in the plan. How did this man change my mind? I didn't have to marry him, since I was pursuing my degree, content and satisfied in my current state. So, why? Over the years, I've gone over this many times, and I still don't have a definitive answer. My life was completely changed, never to be the same again!

CHAPTER 4

Years later, my husband had a heart attack and was diagnosed with cardiovascular disease. His active life style became a slowed down life style! I became his caretaker for three years. My husband died four days after his March 19th birthday on March 23rd. So on a windy day on March 27th, hours after my husband's funeral services, I was sitting at his gravesite, shivering from the cold wind but showing no real emotion. The normal routine was performed: military gun salute, speech, flag presentation, and final Christian rites.

During these performances, a feeling of relief came over me (before you start judging, hear the story). I felt free for the first time in years. I had been married for fifteen years before my husband passed away at the age of thirty-seven, and for thirteen years, I was an abused wife!

For the first two years of our marriage, I didn't see the monster in him until many months later. He had a double personality that had been hidden from me. The first time he slapped me, I was so shocked that I made an excuse for him. I thought he hit me because I had told him that he was drinking too much! Excuse turned into excuse, and the slaps turned into fists and body slams! But as my grandmother used to say, "You can dress a buzzard to look like a peacock, but as soon as the wind blows the feathers off, you'll see it's still the buzzard."

My husband was jealous and a womanizer, and he drank too much! He also became obsessed with beating me. It seemed that he enjoyed inflicting pain on me and then looking at the bruises and swelling!

How could someone do that and then say they're sorry, only to do it all over again and again? Soon, the lies and the cheating became too much to handle and endure.

The blows were so unexpected. He would hit me like he was hitting a man. I never knew if the next argument would put me in the hospital, or maybe worse, if it would be my last. (I was five feet, four inches, weighing 140 pounds, and my husband was six feet, one inch, at 180 pounds!)

I wanted him to stop hurting me. I wanted him to understand that his behavior tore me apart, inside and out.

CHAPTER 5

One day, one of my friends in whom I confided said to me, "If you work through the pain instead of trying to avoid it, you limit the chances of your feelings coming back to haunt you later. Use crying as an outlet, if you must, but whatever you do, find a way to relieve the pain. Don't hold it in." She said that to me because she saw that I was desperate to do something...anything!

Sometimes we are expected to be strong when we're dealing with tough situations. I found that to be ineffective, because the more I tried to hold in my pain and be strong, the worse I felt, and I eventually stressed myself out.

Every day, we have choices: we can move forward with purpose, or we can stay buried in the past. But whatever you choose, set your standards, have goals, take action, work hard, and rise to meet your goals. I was determined to meet my goal of getting my PhD and following my dream of becoming a clinical psychologist. However, my plans of attending my first year of pursuing my MS degree were halted, because I would go to work and school with black eyes and swollen lips! My husband was a man who was more concerned with how I looked to everyone than how I felt after the beatings!

Whatever choices we make in life, there are consequences for them. I used to tell my children about choices. Every decision you make has an impact on someone else. I should have taken my own advice! The only good thing that came from my marriage, as I saw it, was the birth of my children. I love them dearly and would go to all lengths to protect them, and in many cases, I took the beatings my husband wanted to give them—especially my son! My son would be sitting on the floor watching TV, and instead of embracing him, my husband would kick him with his shoes!

CHAPTER 6

Why did I subject myself and my children to such tyranny? Fear!

Fear flees when you understand that God is for you and not against you. I would always think of Job 13:15 in the Bible, when Job said, "Though they slay me, yet will I trust Him." I have always believed in God, and I'm saved by the Holy Spirit, so it was normal for me to pray over everything and everybody. I believe that God has had angels watching over me all of my life. This has been proven to me over and over again, through His grace and mercy toward me because death was around me every day!

But while I was contemplating how to deal with the fear, something within me said, "Go forward!" And my soul replied, "I'm ready to go and be in peace!"

"Why should I take the time to slow down and go over these last years?" I asked myself. Because God told me to move!

And if you think I am a quitter, well, at the time, I *was* a weak, fearful quitter! Yes, I was tired of the verbal and physical abuse. Yes, I had degrees and was an educated woman. Yes, I was exposed to many things that the average woman would jump to do. Yes, I knew what I *should* have done, but that doesn't mean a thing when you're in a toxic environment...when you're trying with everything you have to maintain your sanity and strength for your children.

You may not share those thoughts with me, and I understand that completely. However, it's hard to slow down and think realistically when whirlwinds are disrupting your life. It's difficult to say no to certain events in order to take the time to think through the past years. "So, why should we do this?" you ask.

Well, I'm glad you asked. Because through reviewing my past years, I've come to realize that I have had the opportunity to learn from my mishaps and mistakes, remember God's faithfulness, and thank God for His goodness.

Reviewing my past years has helped me to remember all that God has done and is doing. Forgive me for stating the obvious, but time is moving forward; it is not slowing down. Time is our most precious commodity, and therefore, we have to take advantage of every moment God gives us.

Each moment we have is a gift from God. These gifts turn into precious memories that are soon forgotten unless we take the time to think on them and remember to ask ourselves, "What have you done to move yourself toward your dreams and goals?" Life is a continuous journey, built step by step. Even if we may sometimes stumble in between the steps, nonetheless, we are still moving!

CHAPTER 7

Sometimes remembering hurts!

Abusive relationships can take many forms; typically, however, they involve a cyclical pattern of abusive events revolving around power and control.

The percentages of abuse victims are higher in women than men, but surprisingly, men can be abused also. They are abused verbally, mentally, and in some instances, physically. However, because of the stigma and bad behavior of other men, these male victims remain silent and resort to covering their pain through anger, drinking, smoking, staying out late, or working overtime. These are men who refuse to assault women, not because they are weak, but because they have a deep respect for women! Therefore, because of society and the perceived idea that these men are not "real" men and because of their social and economic status, they remain silent, and their threatened manhood is not revealed.

Yet, through my experiences, I have found that total personal freedom came when I realized that the abuser only has the power and the meaning that we give them. So, why do we hold on to such pain? Why do we choose to blame everyone and everything, rather than choose to see how our greatest pains can actually be blessings?

What we need to do is cut off the abuser mentally and physically! You may feel pressure to forgive your abuser, either from yourself, your family, or your community. But real forgiveness is done for **your** sake, not the sake of the other person. You can choose not to hold on to the burden of anger toward the other person without allowing him or her back into your life. It's difficult to obtain closure (believe me, I know), which is necessary for healing, unless you sever ties with the person who has abused you.

When you change your perspective and your way of thinking, you will view your pain as a gift (I know you may think I'm crazy). In the Bible, Job was blessed double for his faithfulness and trust in God, but **you** are totally responsible for your experience in life. We have to learn to take joy from the power of that responsibility. I had to **learn to create the life I desired and deserved, regardless of the hurts of the past.** We've all experienced pain, loss, and suffering. Believe it or not, these moments shape who we are. But we can choose *how* they shape us, whether they enable us to embrace our dreams or bind us to the past.

Letting go of someone you care about is definitely difficult to do. I was forced to accept that my relationship with my husband was unhealthy, to say the least. To me, my marriage had become dangerous! Was my husband really worth all of this? No, he wasn't.

And I knew I needed to get him out of my life. Sometimes loving someone just isn't enough if you aren't receiving the same love in return. I had to realize that I deserved better.

CHAPTER 8

Night after sleepless night, I lay awake, replaying the fights in my head. But still, the pain had become too unbearable, and this relationship had become too toxic. Inside, I knew my marriage simply couldn't continue, and if I didn't end things now, I might completely lose myself. So, why was it so hard to let go? Why did it have to hurt so bad? Which was worse, the physical hurt or the mental hurt? Was I paralyzed by the fear of my husband or the fear of the unknown?

When you pray and let God handle it, you come out on top! I was too weak to move, so God moved for me. My husband had a medical condition called cardiomyopathy, and he passed away at age thirty-six from the condition.

I stopped pretending everything was okay! I finally allowed the tears to keep falling until I felt they couldn't fall any longer. It lasted a few weeks, but when it was over, I felt like a new person. The tight feeling in my chest was no longer there. I began to think more clearly and notice that things weren't truly as bad as I had thought they were. I started smiling again. I started noticing the sun shining and the beautiful clouds in the sky. No longer was I in that dark place. I felt like a brand new person.

Instead of trying to be strong, crying can sometimes help us in the healing process. When you consider moments of suffering for their complete effect on your life, you see things from a different perspective. If everything had always been easy, how would I have been different? What lessons would have gone unlearned? What strengths would have gone untapped? **I owe the quality of who I am today to each and every moment of my life, including the painful ones.**

So, why are we here? What are we destined to become, to create, to give? How will we create our most enjoyable life? When you understand your purpose spiritually, you **will live with greater passion and drive,** and you will experience a deeper level of clarity and fulfillment.

I prayed and asked the Father to make changes in my life, because I could not think of any circumstance in a marriage that could justify abuse of any kind, whether emotional, mental, physical, or sexual. And by this, I mean assaulting, threatening, or restraining a person through force, which would include hitting, slapping, punching, beating, grabbing, shoving, biting, kicking, pulling hair, burning, using or threatening the use of weapons, blocking a person from leaving a room or the house during an argument, driving recklessly, or intimidating a person with threatening gestures.

All of this and more happened to me! But by the Grace of God, I'm still here! God the Father said that He would never leave me nor forsake me, and that's exactly what happened.

CHAPTER 9

Most women do not stay in abusive relationships because they like being abused. Nor is it true that only weak, helpless women are caught up in abusive relationships. These are just myths; I know because I'm one of these women.

Many of the women involved in abusive relationships are strong, capable women, but over time, they have been weakened by domestic abuse. In fact, it is often the strongest women who will stay in these relationships the longest, for they are determined not to give up, convinced that they can change or fix their relationship. This is the biggest mistake a person can make when deciding to stay in a relationship in which that person is mistreated.

You have to accept that you are the only person you can control in this world! Unless the other person owns up to their mistakes and shows the desire to get help, they probably won't change. They may promise to change and turn things around, and they may even be genuine about their intentions at that moment. But more than likely, things will stay the same, especially if that person made promises in the past that they didn't fulfill.

Change has to come from within; it cannot be forced. Only then do things have a chance of working themselves out; all the anointed oil on the head and in the shoes and the laying on of hands won't do it. Only God can change the heart of man!

Chapter 10

As an abused wife, I've observed some reasons why a woman does not seek the help she needs and stays with an abusive husband. Some of these may not seem realistic to the average person, but to abused women, they are real!

- She still loves him.
- She feels sorry for him and believes she can help him.
- He promised her that he would get help.
- She feels the good times outweigh the bad.
- She believes if she can work harder to please him, he will treat her better.
- She blames herself and thinks she deserves the beatings.
- She doesn't believe she can escape her abuser's domination.
- She may think other people will believe it's her fault.
- Her abuser threatens to kill her, others, and/or himself if she leaves him.
- She feels she cannot financially support herself and her children.

- She has no other support system available (friends, family, etc.).
- She believes that if she hangs in there with him, things will change and get better.
- She fears being alone.
- She came from an abusive home, so the violence seems natural.
- She denies or minimizes the abuse (i.e., "It really wasn't that bad. He only hits me every few months").
- She stays because of religious or cultural beliefs (i.e., believing she is abandoning God or her parent's values if she leaves).
- She believes leaving will mean she is a failure as a wife and mother.
- She does not know her legal rights and feels she has no options.
- She stays because of the children.
- She doesn't know anywhere she can move or go.
- She is too afraid or feels too powerless to leave.
- He isn't always brutal; he can be very loving when he's not abusive.
- She is unaware of the resources available to her.

Some women stay in the relationship because of the children, not recognizing that the abuse has an impact on them as well. Children from abused homes often have relationship and marital problems as adults. They also can struggle with the concept of God, finding it especially difficult to accept the love of an eternal, heavenly Father.

But I say to you, you do not deserve to be abused, nor are you to blame for the abuse that you have suffered. Abuse of any type is wrong, and if you are in an abusive situation, the first step toward new life and freedom is to recognize that there is a need for a change in your life. Change can be difficult, and in some cases, change can be frightening. However, in any type of an abusive situation, change is absolutely necessary for your own wellbeing.

Unfortunately, most people don't see how bad things are from the outside, even when someone points it out to them. How many years have you lived with a sense of quiet desperation, faking the connection we have with ourselves? Why do we deny ourselves real living and exchange it for mindless living?

Chapter 11

Over the years, life silently and slowly erased my identity.

Life had brought me to a place I had never been before. I could no longer silence the cries of my quiet desperation, the yearning to break free from what everyone wanted me to be. Everyone (family and friends) wanted me to be the loyal submissive wife in a loving home that they envisioned! Sometimes we can be so busy trying to please everyone else we forget our own identity.

During my entire situation of abuse, I immersed myself in the church. Every chance I got, I was in the church doing something to take my mind off of what was to come.

If you are not attending a Christ-centered church with a strong, Bible-teaching ministry, now is the time to begin finding one. The church can help you in several ways. It can offer you love and emotional support, spiritual counseling (individual, marital, and family), food and shelter, financial support, and guidance.

In the past, many churches were not equipped to handle the problem of domestic abuse, perhaps because of a lack of education about the problem, a lack of resources, or an unwillingness to admit that abuse exists in Christian homes. However, more and more churches are recognizing the need for this type of ministry and are learning how to deal with abuse biblically.

The next option for you would be to find a Christian counselor with experience in the area of abuse, or a licensed counselor outside of the church. But wherever you go, *go!*

After the death of my husband, I decided to take some time off mentally for myself. I had four children to raise, and I felt that I couldn't do it alone. So, I knelt down in my living room and asked God to take me and give me the spiritual and mental knowledge that would enable me to raise my children alone with His help.

Sometimes it seems like the end of the world, even though it's not.

Your mind can attempt to play tricks on you, making you believe that happiness isn't possible any longer. But that isn't true. Often, the best cure for pain is time.

By resting your heart, mind, and soul, you give yourself a chance to heal. This is also the best time to get to know yourself. Maybe there's a hobby that you love or an activity you enjoy doing. For me, it was baking. Even though baking didn't completely take my mind off of things, it allowed me to spend time alone doing something I really enjoyed, and I appreciated that. Eventually, I began focusing more on myself and less on my situation. I began to finish what I started—I went back to school.

Going back to school didn't work immediately, but over time, it helped a lot. If you allow it, each day will become a little easier. Time heals. And even though my relationship didn't work out as planned, I realized I could still enjoy my life. Happiness is within your control!

After abuse, your life isn't over, because taking back control begins with you.

Everyone needs help in life at one time or another. You don't have to go through overcoming abuse alone. I am living proof that you **can** get through this. **You can overcome your situation by resting your heart, mind, and soul. You have to give yourself a chance to heal. This is also the best time to get to know yourself** (I am purposely repeating this).

My soul constantly yearns to be in harmony with my mind and heart. These three facets of my identity are vital and crucial to my wellbeing.

Let's face it: there will be very demanding days when you are doing so many things, and the hustle of life can get complicated, but in order to regain your self-esteem, you must take time for your soul to rest. Everything and everyone needs downtime. During this time in my life, I needed rest badly!

Denying the fact that I was living under a darkness of desperation led me to a realization about my life. Sometimes in the lowest points of our lives, when all seems to be falling apart, life is actually falling into place.

When the walls are caving in, the air is getting scarce, and you feel like you're at your last breath, something amazing happens. Your pain transforms, your agony evolves into something bigger, and you realize that a new you is about to emerge.

My desperation was the pathway to rediscovering my inspiration. The dark valley in which I found myself led me to higher grounds. Now, I don't push away the struggles or hide from hard times. Instead, I remain patient, allowing the pain to bring forth a new chapter in my life. Sometimes you need to take a few steps back in order to take giant leaps forward.

Today, I seek to stay centered. While centered, I feel most alive and the happiest.

Now, I can thank the years of desperation I lived, for I am now on the path to living life as the best version of myself. I have not allowed all of the negativeness I have experienced to weaken my faith. They have strengthened me more to understand that God only lets us go through what was in His plan. My situation of abuse was a distinct moment in His plan. I live in His plan every day.

CHAPTER 12

Ecclesiastes 3:1 – "To everything there is a season, A time for every purpose under heaven."

O ur condition or the condition of our situation does not limit God...

Our **when** (or our timing) and our connectedness to the timing of the miraculous in our lives is what determines our situation.

Someone said, "I'll praise God *when* I feel like it," or, "I'll praise God *when* He does something for me..."

Well, we live in a world of *when's. When* we are born, *when* we die, *when* we build, *when* we tear down...

In the second chapter of the book of Acts, the Scripture tells us that "*when* the day of Pentecost was fully come...there came a sound from Heaven."

Understand there is a *when* in God's timing.

There is a *when* in His plan for our lives.

There is a *when* in the incidents and even the tragedies that make up the events of our lives.

God did not necessarily plan these events to happen. But, to a large degree, they happened as the result of chance. They happened at a distinct moment and at a particular point of change in our life.

There is a *when* to it all. My question to us today is, what will we do with our *when*? Keep in mind that my *when* may be different from yours, but we all have a *when*.

When we are in the valley, we experience problems and situations that only God can solve, because sometimes there is danger in trying to solve our problems in our own way. So, while we're in the valley, God is teaching us how to handle the difficulties and disappointments of life—the healing, the hurt, the tears, the heartaches, the pain, and the loneliness. But when He has put the finishing touch on us, we will come out with the spirit of love, joy, peace, and happiness!

There is a timing of it all, you see. What will we do with the moment of interruption in our lives when we feel God's presence or the unction of His Spirit in our lives, or that moment when God reaches out to us, or that moment when we should be reaching out to Him?

Think about when we have been in a really bad situation...

The family was really sick.

It didn't look like the marriage was going to last.

She was about to give up.

He just lost his job.

Her car just broke down.

The rent was due.

Doctors, attorneys, and marriage counselors couldn't help any more. Who would have thought there was hope for the situation? Who would have thought it could turn out the way that it did? But someone decided to praise Him! Somebody found a *when* to Worship in the midst of his or her tragedy.

You see, David was a worshipper. He didn't need a whole lot of prompting to get him to lift his hands or worship the Lord! The circumstances in David's life were not going to determine the *when* of his worship to God. David was capable of cutting out a moment of his life regardless of his circumstances and creating a "*when* opportunity" for God's timing in his life.

He could have reacted the way most people would have. He could have forgotten God's ability to help him, and he could have just gone into battle by himself, without God. Instead, David decided that it was better to go into battle with a praise to God on his lips, rather than a curse from the Amalekites.

Understand, at this moment of his life, the timing of David's praise meant everything. He didn't praise God after the battle, and He didn't even praise God before the battle. David's *when* was right in the middle of the thing that was trying to destroy not only his family, but even his own life.

We say, "Well, I'll praise God later, or, "I'll praise God when this thing is all over," or, "I'll praise God after this storm of life has ended."

You must realize that God inhabits the praises of His people. In other words, He shows up *when* we worship Him.

So, our perspective should not be, "Hey, look over there. God just showed up, so now we will all go to praising Him." Instead, we should say, "Hey, we want God to show up, so we go to praising Him."

God inhabits the praises of His people! If you need Him to show up in your situation, begin praising Him. Know that it's important for us to comprehend the *when* of God's timing in our lives.

In Acts 16, Paul and Silas:

Heal a young woman who is possessed with a demon.

Are falsely accused after the people turn on them.

Are stripped of their clothes and beaten severely.

Are cast into the inner part of the prison.

Have their hands and feet fastened with iron shackles and chains.

It looked like this was a *what* situation for Paul and Silas. They could have complained and said, "Look at *what's* happened to us. Look at *what* they have done! *What* did we do to deserve this?"

But instead of complaining, they started singing, praying, and praising God.

When you look at your life, your situation may look like a *what* situation to you and everyone around you, but it may very well be a *when* situation to God.

God gives all of us a *when* moment to thank and praise Him. No matter what you are facing, you should praise Him because He has done something for you.

CHAPTER 13

B ut the *when* for me is not after He has done something.

The *when* for me is before I even have a need! I could very well have a pity party for myself and say, "Where was God when my life was turned upside down?" But I had a choice, and I chose Jesus!

When my husband was brutally abusing me and I didn't think I would make it, God was there!

When I had shingles, He was there! *When* I had pneumonia, He was there! *When* I had breast cancer, He was there! *When* I had diabetes, He was there! *When* I was diagnosed with heart disease, He was there! *When* I was diagnosed with vascular disease, He was there! *When* I was diagnosed with kidney disease, He was there! *When* they thought I had a stroke, He was there! *When* I had congestive heart failure, He was there! *When* I had spinal stenosis, He was there! *When* I was in a diabetic coma, He was there!

Your praise is not just about where you are, nor is it about the circumstances of your situation. It's about the timing of your worship.

God still moves mountains, He still keeps His eye on the storm, and He is still in charge of our every movement!

I want to thank Him for life! I want my experiences to be a testimony that will help someone wake up, get up, and start over.

Why do I praise God so much? Because through all that I've endured, He has never left me! He has kept my mind and my life! He made me a new person. Even though I was down and lowly in body and spirit, He gave me the strength to get up and start the new life that I was ordained and destined to have!

So, I got up and started living again! **I am a survivor! I survived the storm! You can and will begin again!**

Why am I being so transparent? Because I want to be right and ready when the miraculous happens!

No more fear of the unknown, no more fear of people, because the fears of this earth are not to be compared to the fear of God that we should have. Jesus said, "Take courage, I am with you... Trust Me!" (Matt. 14:27).

Chapter 14

Practice gratitude. As a survivor of abuse, it can be hard to find things to be grateful for. It may even seem wrong or perverse to focus on gratitude after you have been hurt so deeply.

However, several studies suggest that focusing on what you are grateful for in life can have a healing effect for victims of trauma. These effects take time to see. One study showed that it took an average of eight months for gratitude to produce any positive impact.

Practicing gratitude doesn't mean that you ignore the suffering you have experienced. Instead, it means that you choose to honor the fact that you have survived this trauma. It means that you are taking a moment to reflect on your environment and what it's doing to enrich your spiritual life. We all need a spiritual life! You are strong.

Being grateful for your ability to survive and cope can help you build a psychological "immune system" against future stresses and trauma. Practicing gratitude doesn't mean you'll always *feel* grateful. You can't control how you feel. Even if you don't feel it, try practicing gratitude through actions such as recording good memories or positive moments in a journal, or having positive and fun conversations. Perhaps even write a book (like me)!

There are times when running away from something takes more courage than staying in it! It takes more courage to remove yourself from an environment that encourages you to remain hurt and fearful, to think sinful thoughts, and to continuously do the wrong things. It takes more courage to walk away from a fight than to raise your fists; it takes more courage to keep your mouth shut than to return a curse; it takes more courage to walk out of a bar, to put down the drink, to put out the cigarette, to walk away from the dime bag, or to say no to a midnight bootie call.

Whatever the reasons, whatever the circumstances, it takes courage to walk away from them.

A spiritual life is very comforting and rewarding, for it helps us to live out our potential in the way that God intended for us.

What happens to you is premised on how you live, who you live with, and how you spend your time. What you allow your mind to receive determines the atmosphere in which you live. Don't expect apples to fall from a peach tree!

Healing from domestic abuse can have lasting effects on your mental, physical, and emotional health! Survivors, like myself, may suffer from low-self-esteem or feelings of panic and helplessness, and if you have medical conditions, they can aggravate these symptoms. But be patient with yourself and remember, you are not alone!

Clarify what "it" is in this situation.

Have a Great Day,
Doretha John

CPSIA information can be obtained
at www.ICGtesting.com
Printed in the USA
BVHW091052160921
616889BV00017B/1182